Edge & Cusp

Other Work by Richard Lister

Non-Fiction

Flourish: Fuller life for all through Church and Community Transformation - Regnum Books, 2022

RICHARD LISTER

EDGE & CUSP

First published in paperback format by
Coverstory books, 2022

ISBN 978-1-7397660-0-9

© Richard Lister 2022

The right of Richard Lister to be identified as the author of this work has been asserted by him in accordance with the Copyright, Designs and Patents Act 1988.

The cover photograph was taken by Richard Lister and the cover designed by Eleanor Lister © 2022.

All rights reserved.

No part of this publication may be reproduced, circulated, stored in a system from which it can be retrieved, or transmitted in any form without the prior permission in writing of the publisher.

www.coverstorybooks.com

Contents

Part 1
Painting with darkness and light 7
Breath 8
Alight 10
First time 11
Your foot in my hands 12
Taking your time 13
Logmore Green 15
Mutation 16
Awake 17
Bluebell and Leaf 18

Part 2
Fillide's Tale 21
Life in the Red 23
Solitary 24
Periphery 26
Traveller 27
Is this my home 29
Malawi, Famine, Gunshot 30
Nomad 31
Your home 32
Seeing Colour 33

Part 3
Beyond the scene 37
Hidden 38
A peculiar pint 39
Motherwell's Muse 40
Blurred edges 42
Riddle from the sands 43
Emerald fate 45
Surreal, with vulture 47
Cruising the juju of leisure 48
Singed Whiskers and Coffee 49

Part 4
Caravaggio never painted 53
Melancholy 55
Shoelace of thought 56
Six suited men 58
One good foot 59
Held 60
Skull Talks 62
A pew, a pillar and you 63
One sack for Sigele 65
Of touch 67

❊

Acknowledgements 71

For Ellie, Tom and Ollie, who bring such joy to my life.

Part 1

Painting with darkness and light

Caravaggio knows the dark; don't we all?
For him, it's Rome's seething underside:
scarce-cooked horse-meat, stench of dung,
tallow candles spitting like cats. Fillide's
hard face and her soft tongue, the shudder
of his blade as it skewers his rival's life.
Banishment. His self-portrait is a cry for grace
but what light is there in Rome?

Rembrandt's *Portrait as the apostle Paul*
reveals that life has flowed,
with grit, across his face. A ridged forehead,
sagging cheeks, deep, dull eyes. They show
a man who's been spurned by art's fickle fashion,
has pawned his painter's props for soup
and left a rose and tears on the grave of Saskia,
his wife. Yet, the background is dark earth tones,

not just bone black, and there's warm light falling
on his head. It highlights white and yellow-gold
spun in his swept hat. The artist shows his face,
as vulnerable as ours. Rembrandt's mysterious
depths have 'said things for which there are no
words in any language'. He paints the Bible
like it's true: full of washerwomen, beggars, the blind
and a God who hugs a wayward son.

The quote in the final stanza is a comment by Van Gogh on Rembrandt.

Breath

Rabbit, your right eye looks into mine.
You quiver with *nephesh*,
it fizzes in your 10g brain,
skitters around your heart.

The lower half of your face
moves non-stop as you chew
a gruel-thin supper of grass.
Your fur, part-blown like an old sofa;

tall sculpted ears, sifting the wind;
molten toffee eye.
I breathe in a drift of air
that you've breathed out.

My life beats slower than yours,
a bell tolling for a time;
my skin no longer taut;
right ankle hobbled.

You think of me
(with my predator's eyes)
in spark-fast thoughts,
a twitch from flight.

Yet we're both made from clay,
wet with God's spittle,
moulded by his fingers
for this, our fugitive life.

You are spooked
by my car's rumble
and leap for your hole,
are clipped by a rear wheel.

Next morning I drag myself
back to the site, hoping
you're not still alive,
half-squashed into the tarmac.

Your guts are blown out
like an egg sac, legs rigid,
eyes pecked clean.
'Sorry. Sorry'.

I pick you up,
cast you over the fence,
away from the road:
feels more dignified.

By afternoon, just hawthorn,
bullied by the wind;
your hole, spills of earth;
grass, so bright it hurts.

Nephesh is the Hebrew word for living being, that which has breath.

Alight

A line as delicate
as a spider's sigh defines
the edges of this pansy.
Eight imperial purple strokes
draw the eye. Beyond sight
ultraviolet landing lights have enticed
an Early-Nesting Bumblebee,
his hairy body perfect for cold
spring air. He dips his proboscis
and sips, nectar scaled to his tongue.

First time

Today, for the first time in twenty years, I put on
your blue jumper. I'm in the garden wrestling with
the spent roots of bell heather and lavender.
100% acrylic, it's long since breathed out

from a 42" chest. Made in Italy, back when.
I remember you wearing it with bonfire smoke
drifting across you, clouds on the flank
of Etive Mor. I imagine this smoke, my favourite smell,

is curled, like a dragon's tail, deep around the fabric.
Our neighbour, Tony, wobbles slightly
as he comes to greet me. He too is wearing
a worn-down sweater. Tony's over ninety now,

so is your vintage. He has cheeks as sharp
as a rock face, a bent stook of hair and pendulous ears.
I find my blood filling with warmth for I see
that he'll try his stroke-cracked words with me.

He takes out his upper set of teeth,
set in pink plastic and wet with saliva,
to tell me about the purple crocuses that grace his garden.
His eyes reflect the early spring sun.

Your ashes were scattered by the roots of a silver birch.
I've never seen this tree. But I know that it drew in
the last dust of you to form its sap and bark.
It would be your birthday soon.

Your foot in my hands

You chose to cut off one toe
because it curled into
the roof of your shoe.
The rest are purple.

Your toenails are the
ochre of Saxon bones,
bent back and inward,
too twisted to be trimmed.

I gently knead the sole
of your right foot,
feel the dryness of your skin
and, beneath, a glassy cold;

try to weave warmth
back into your flesh,
to smudge at least
one source of pain.

'If I was a cat I'd purr'
you say, 'do feel free to stop'
but I stay cross-legged
on this lilac carpet

honoured to rub
your feet, such a small
thing for all those years,
a gift.

Taking your time

Sunlight clips a stick,
spills a shadow
on a sundial's plate.
It's etched with hours;
the day's been caught
and sliced.

A bell, flicked into song
by mechanical clock,
cracks sleep,
draws Anselm,
snail slow, into the Abbey:
night's prayer begins.

Edison's electric
bulb pushes
back the night,
tricks with its light,
conjures work
from time to sleep.

Anne's thumbs flutter
as the film's pace drops.
Multi-tasks with phone.
Megapixels spit.
Dopamine hits.
Hurried.

Common Banded Snail,
shell of calcium carbonate
like a curled stalactite
of scratched white
and luscious brown,
chews on a nettle leaf.

One tentacle, topped
with a minute eye,
telescopes upward,
slow as the rising sun,
reaches out
into an untamed world.

Logmore Green

Coppice hazels strain
towards the sky;
two pigeons clatter into flight.
The field beyond is empty:

no rabbits sortie out
to graze. Myxomatosis
filled them with fever,
led them lethargic

into death.
Foxes, slink-low
in the grass, became
just ribcages, then less.

Today, beside the track,
a slice of sheet piling,
twisted as if soft
as chewing gum

and a gutted car chassis,
rust-brown axle and springs.
Men have dumped them at night.
I sense a twitch beside my feet:

a bronze Slow Worm,
like a Celtic bracelet
charmed to sluggish life
to glitter on this edge.

Mutation

Puffballs trace
a delicate arc,
a calligraphic character
that's seeped up
from the soil.

Light dissolves,
the chestnut trees
in Bushy Park
begin to blend
with thorn and grass
and woad-blue lake.

The scene is wrecked.
Polluted. Tainted
by a lump:
a plastic bag.

'How dare they chuck that!'
A youth strides after his bulldog
but does not stop.
'Does no-one care?'

Closer up I start
to see the bag
cannot keep its lines,
is melting shape.

Four simple curves
outline a swan,
head snuggled in,
asleep.

Awake

A thin place
where beauty aches
from the palest snow
and the line of peaks
cuts sharply into the air.

The moment of nonchalance
skimming like a slate
from dip, to crest, down
a sweep of slope
ruffled with powdered sky

to shush, tucked down,
awake to every bump
the chance to catch a ski
to spill and break
yet never quite.

And do all this with you,
this is to carve the edge
of breath and glow.
To swoop through woods
bright with sun-dressed ice,

to dream that mud and rock
aren't true, that messages
can carry through the gaps
from there to here
and settle as new snow.

Bluebell and Leaf

I breathe in nothing
but clear air till I sense
a drift of bluebell,
heady and redolent
of past and peace.

A fly passes, absorbed
in its tunnel of sound
and in the canopy
robin and great tit call,
like singing stars.

Sweeps of bluebell
smudge the margin
of mauve and ultramarine;
the flowers stand, tang sharp,
against their fresh leaves.

Yet wonder is not caught
in these alone: the floor's
a weave of pallid leaves
made fine by autumn's death
in traceries and swirls.

I sit on a tumbled branch,
try not to fill my mind
but seek in all this beauty
the stillness beyond my sight,
the *Abba* voice of God.

Part 2

Fillide's Tale
'Salome with the head of John the Baptist' by Caravaggio

Caravaggio always painted me,
or so he said. Did he
love me? I ... don't know,
he gave me gifts, a twist
of satin scarf dark as the cracks

in a blacksmith's face.
And a tilted beeswax candle,
smelt of sweet hay and honey,
most likely swiped from a church.
But was that just a boast,

for *fama* in front of his gang?
He yearned for me, most men did
when I was as ripe as *burrata*.
His eyes savoured me as I modelled
for him and then, more than his eyes.

We whispered touch for my *pappone*
Tomassoni was bred from bile.
Yet I saw how Caravaggio's hand
lingered on a man's cheek:
he dipped his feet in both pools.

There was something cracked in him,
like me he'd grown up quick,
been clouted by the horse-kick of life.
You see, his father died of plague.
We were both from north of Rome,

he teased me for my Sienna accent:
the way I said *chiacchierare*.
I saw this painting. Scipio Borghese,
the Pope's nephew, held it curtained off.
Perhaps Scipio is Herod - with neat goatee:

all the muscles of power, none of the guts;
could have saved him, didn't care.
John the Baptist's haggard head,
untended hair and beard,
that's Caravaggio's. After he killed

Tomassoni they made him
bando capitale, pitched him
into exile. His profile
looks weary; to die is rest.
The shadows are bone black.

Look at Salome's egg-shaped face
and you see me. Her white sash
cannot staunch the blood.
She turns her face away.
How could she bear that prize?

---

fama: renown or reputation; *pappone*: pimp;
burrata: cheese made from mozzarella and cream;
chiacchierare: to chat; *bando capitale*: banished on pain of death.

Life in the Red
Mumbai, India

These women are young,
their faces taut
and salwar kameez dull from use.
Three carry babies
tucked on their backs,
blood-beat close.

I say *Namaste*,
lean back against a wall.
The ceiling fan groans
as it curls the heat.
Aesha leads
four *Magahi* songs,

shares how to protect
yourself from syphilis
and hands round biscuits,
crumbled in one corner.
Kavita, who smells faintly
of garam masala, stays behind.

She says 'I grew
into a spindly girl in Bihar',
India's ground-down state.
'My Auntie told me
of hotel work for good rupees'.
She tiptoed on the burnished steps,

was trafficked to this slum
and forced into a different
trade: brutal nightly abuse.
'Will you pray for me
and the child I bear?'
My words falter, we slowly weep.

Solitary
Angkor Watt, Cambodia, 1994

She's prostrate before Vishnu:
ten feet tall in chipped sandstone,
eight arms, somnolent eyes.
Kneeling with her chest

and face pressed deep into
the floor. Her right hand
holds a lock of hair, ragged cut;
she places it at the statue's feet.

What burdens bring her here,
alone? An empty womb,
uncle spitting spots of blood,
rice crop rank with blight?

She ignored Ta Prohm,
the temple that the forest
fights with roots that tear
the uninvited stone.

Threaded past Bayon's giant
heads that stare out east,
holding in their thoughts;
she's silent as a moth.

The light begins to slur,
trees melt, shadows pool.
She needs to retreat.
Each morning, state soldiers

hold this place. Each evening,
the Khmer Rouge regain
the ground - by strange
agreement, like two cats, who

knowing each other's routes,
choose to never overlap.
She slips between
the twilight and her pain.

Periphery
Khartoum

He has a face.
Burned umber or ebony.
Scuffle of beard.
I think he's wearing a white top,
maybe a shirt.
He has one leg, I know that,
and at least one questing hand.

The bush somewhere in South Sudan.
Thorny acacia, tufts of finger-grass.
A click. The endless now.
Pupils dilate, blood pours to legs
so he can run.
No more.

A crumpled iron shack
in eastern Khartoum before dawn.
He's cooking kisra flatbread
in a pan puddled with grease.
Takes it off the flame,
gives two pieces of bread
to the boy in the corner, eats one.
A bullet case falls from his pocket, bounces and rolls.
The mongrel outside snarls.

Is he saying something?
Arabic. Guttural.
I am pressed between him
and braids of cars
washing down this side street.
He hops closer.
Should I stop, share tattered dollars
or hurry out before that van?
I step out, I never see.

Traveller

hands black with grease,
knuckles scuffed, skin
as tough as tent canvas.

He stands on the edge
as I slam my bumper car
into a pretty girl's

with a tangle of sparks
and wafts of burnt rubber.
I grip the wheel

with my right hand, clean
except for a blue ink stain
on my middle finger.

My palm, translucent,
mottled cream and pink;
nails clipped in straight lines.

He sees 'Surrey Boy',
kitted in a striped white jumper,
unsullied, unearned -

bought with an allowance -
a boy who must look down
on a circus lad.

I see a reputation:
learned from a single tale
at our kitchen table.

One gypsy barked a cough
as his mate filched
cigarettes and a coke

from the corner shop
on Portsmouth Road.
Or so they thought.

I exit the bumper car,
blood trilling, neck sore.
'Cheers' as I pass him,

heading for candyfloss.
No more words:
our myths remain untouched.

Is this my home
Malawi, 2001

… though I have never been here?
Beneath the plane, the landscape of button huts
and grass-blade palms is easing itself, as we descend,
into somewhere large enough to work and live.

In Zomba, I will turn left at the forked mango tree,
edge the dented Corolla round the rocks
to reach a whitewashed house: reassuring
mosquito net, ceramic water filter,

Serotine bats in the roof. Sheets of memories
will transmute this brick and corrugated iron
into my home. Eating gritty *nsima* by hand
with Yakobe, *Yes Prime Minister* on tape

and a chameleon tightrope-walking
along the washing line. And yet my roots
are not here. Nor in the neo-Georgian
house blanks of childhood Camberley.

Even the beckoning scarp and dip
of the South Downs, which draws in
my breath, cannot hold me for I know
I am a stranger without roots.

Malawi, Famine, Gunshot

jerks us awake.
2am. Pupils gape, breath still.
Silence.

'Why's our dog not barking?
Is he dead?'
Nothing.

Our mosquito net
no longer feels like safety,
just flimsy gauze,

the bolted kitchen door
won't last long
against a gang of hungry men with guns.

Silence.
'Where's Yakobe?'

Our guard
curls up in the diesel-black dark
beyond the papaya tree;

his machete,
with which he deftly
slices air and grass,

won't help much.
'Keep still, Yakobe.'

I ring my boss' house.
'Code red'.
Silence.

Nomad
England

November 1986.
I walk down Crawley Hill
and flit through cadmium-yellow
cones of lamppost light. Inside,
I sit on a worn armchair

talking with George Lawton,
about sixty with a jowly face,
a man I hardly know.
Our conversation starts
with the dangers of a game

and moves steadily inward
until his challenge with its seams
of grace. As he prays
'we welcome you, Holy Spirit'
I realise, to my surprise,

that there's an unseen
presence in the room,
a quiet authority, clean
as sunlight at dawn.
I am filled with warmth.

And so, for the first time,
I encounter you, my God.
More real than granite,
hewn from love. You,
who wrap yourself with light

like a cloak, call me by name
to live for you. I realise I am
now a nomad in this life.
Yet, each night I'll pitch
my threadbare tent nearer home.

Your home
Brazil

I am shocked by your scarlet face,
pupils obscure as crazed glass,
hair blending into moonless night.
Imp, satyr, Bacchus himself?

Yet your head is tilted, like you're
listening to a friend. There is a patience
in your eyes, as if you're waiting
for a photographer's umpteenth click.

Behind the trickles of face paint
you have no twisted horns. On Facebook
President Bolsanaro declared
'Indians are undoubtedly changing…

they are increasingly becoming
human beings just like us.'
Paulo Guajajara is your name.
Guajajara is your tribe: owners

of the feathered head ornament.
Master of ze'egete, the good speech,
Guardian of the Forest and father.

You say 'These people
think they can come here,
into our home, and help themselves
to our forest? No!

We won't allow it. We don't break
into their houses and rob them, do we?'

One week later, five loggers,
spiny with guns, will ambush you:
ten bullets will rip out your life.

Seeing Colour
Nepal

The River Ratu slides
wide, slow
between its gentle banks
and there,

a splash of brown in red,
she walks with grace.
Slender, she places her feet,
toes spread on sand, no mark.

I, a patch of white
in red, walk up,
colour box in hand
to sit and paint.

I guess her home is thatched,
has sugar, salt and spice,
this place for drink,
a song for light.

My skills, all abstract
academic lines,
I could not weave
or plait or thread.

My looks and English words
are ragged nets for living here;
Gurung, her tongue,
is hook and fish.

Slender, she places her feet,
toes spread on sand, no mark.

Part 3

Beyond the scene
'Sick Bacchus' by Caravaggio

What makes me pause?
I, the god of revels,
am not in the dance,
sit on my own, shoulder
in moonlight, my gaze
drifted down, thinking.

My face is fish-pale,
tinged with green.
I've held lead-white,
breathed in vermillion's
poisoned scent,
drunk deep to cover

painter's cholic, and in
its grip taken to the night:
Rome's underworld.
Brash fellows in a gang,
a glance taken amiss
and blood lets rip.

Yet. I am here;
alone. The grapes I hold
too few for ecstasy.
My time is meant for
more: to tease out the light
through flesh and skin.

Can I rejoin the dance
with swirling twisted vine
and step between
the shadows and the flame?
The *chiaroscuro* line,
of sacred and profane.

Hidden
скрытый
1961

in wild garlic
red hair dashed with grey
remove soil
military pass
or dirt

Tsvetnoy Boulevard
shake dry
belted raincoat
tear leaves

briefly greet puff-cheeked Janie
chop
and give this child
pungent

tin of sweets
bear leek
with faint motes of Leila tobacco
pinch of pepper

walk on
pinenuts
the girl passes the package
fuse

to her mother in a cerise polka dot scarf
taste
drops it into the hood of her pram
season

box jammed with four rolls of microfilm
seal
missile positions in Cuba
freeze

A peculiar pint
Hunter's Inn, Devon 1942

He holds a pint of Blue Lobster,
pauses as if counting beats,
puffs back the fleece of froth, sips
and settles. Shortish back-and-sides,

pale face, pockmarked
like a fraction of the moon.
The barman asks 'anything to eat?'
'No I ate ... yes, something sweet',

the 'th' flattened just a tad. He takes
the bag of pear drops, pays,
heads out the door. No fuss.
The barman never sees him

doubleback; splash along the stream
to Heddon's Mouth; row into the sea,
kissed with stars; slip into a U Boat turret;
resume command.

Motherwell's Muse

I cross from New York's
Sunday-softened streets
into the Guggenheim Museum
and fall in size until

I am but the few draft
lines that populate a sketch
that's focused on a building's
shape and space and flow.

Step into a gallery and stop,
like a smashed watch.
Vast canvas.
A Motherwell.

Three dark and ragged ovals,
each unique: the tall, the thin,
the fat, on a ground of white and tan,
blocked in by massive columns.

'Elegy to the Spanish Republic, no.110',
a lifelong series of lament;
strange theme for an American
who never saw Spain.

Motherwell as a cod-pale boy
stumbles from Californian waves,
his lungs rasping, gasping at insufficient air:
death becomes his muse, and grows.

When the artist is 21,
Spain detonates into civil war:
neighbour stabbing neighbour,
people with the faces of God tumbled

into mass graves like carcasses
with plague. He pares it all back
to the black husks of lives
and the searing white sun.

Blurred edges

Slurped at my feet
by the last wave.
Obscuring a circle of sand,

a common moon jellyfish,
like a mirage with the confusion
of a creature with no

head or eyes,
brain, blood or heart, it drifts
with the current even when swimming.

Its tentacle venom is vicious
to plankton
that get snagged.

So: prone to blending in, poor swimmer, with a tendency to sting.
Two thirds of our genome - identical.

Riddle from the sands

Stay,
I didn't mean it when I said
you were gross,
condensed,
crude

but you move,
full of breath,
in your solid, clunky world
that blares with turquoise,
emerald, madder,

it makes me sick.
You must understand
how I feel
with my soles
and yours chained

with rust and slipper-limpet shells
and you, carefree,
care less.
You drag me wherever you pick,
loom over me,

yank me into the rock's shade
so I faint out.
Yet. You could be
so much more.
Join me,

let go the grizzled anchors,
allow yourself to disperse
until you're free
to shrink at noon to watch unseen,
stretch across this beach,

shimmy the cliff.
It'd be a fine exchange.
You'd see anew,
within the line,
the flat,
the keen.

So stay.
For us.
With your back to the sun
till it leaks out
and I pray for a changeling moon.

Emerald fate

       Pagóni, your peacock eye, leftover shard of night,
             with cold, clear sight sank a barb in me.

          I left the carcass of the deer,
            its warmth waning,
              scurried up the rocks but
              you were gone.
                   One token feather remained
             by the banyan roots
              traced with an eye for luck, like a skiff.

    Back here, in a pale courtyard in Babylon,
   I am slathered in sweat,
  crave water, not wine.
The arrow wound
in my breast still sighs out blood.
   Gods - why have you cursed me?

   I, Alexander, who unleashed war,
     phalanx spears sweeping
        into faces of boiling hate - or fear.
     Ploughs lie unhitched, hair unkissed,
all for your honour in Olympus.

Am I not a god like you, Heracles,
    bile of your bile, but you abandon me?
        Am I not a god?

            And yet I saw you, pagóni,
              in the dawn before the battle.
                  Sweet messenger, in ripples of lapiz,
                   fan unfurled, fresh with emerald.

At the Indian river I fought their king
in black rain gouged with lightning.
A war elephant with savaged ear
skewered my friend Barak on its tusk.
My men would go no further.

With my chest in flame,
I see you, pagóni, one last time.
You fix me with a cry as sharp as shattered bone.
You call the dead to dine in Hades - so call me now.

pagóni is ancient Greek for a peacock

Surreal, with vulture
The Darfur conflict, Sudan 2009

A Nubian vulture tracks us
as we play volleyball
inside the Catholic compound.
We're vaguely safe here.

He's high in an acacia thorn-tree
with smart black feathers
so we make him our umpire.
His neck is naked pink.

We need him to rule
on who gets the point
when the ball is tipped down
by the looping phone line.

Francis, from Gabon, is all
domed biceps and sleek legs,
his teammates slam
with butter-slick ease.

When they duff a pass
they jest and jostle:
'you total fool' or
'can't you even play?'

My team scrambles,
thin-legged and scrappy.
Paolo, in full black cassock,
shunts the ball into the net.

Our umpire flaps off,
in no particular hurry.

Cruising the juju of leisure

Cheap enough to drop: an actor damaged
by his past, its ropes and wires and spiky heels
on wooden floors. He smokes untipped,

his tea is deep brown like clay and everything
- the purple lights, copper pipes, and alabaster -
is sucked into the centre, the stage itself.

He makes a division between the auditorium
of velvet and gilt and the rest of the cruise ship
with its free drinks and steep walls.

Life is a basket of logs needing to be replenished
and, at a time like this, you exclusively deserve it.
Beyond the small window glass and iron gate

immerse yourself in Belgrade,
Arbanasi, Novi Sad.
Disembark and transfer cigarettes.

Discover the airing cupboard of Croatia,
the microwave of a village brimming with history.
Who could not be obsessed with the juju

of leisure when time is as limited as dry kindling?
It's the romance of a front door:
beautiful enough to keep forever.

Found Poetry drawing from '*The White Road: A Journey into Obsession*' Edmund de Waal (2015);
'Essential Reading' for The Old Priory Self Catering Cottage; '*Being an actor*' Simon Callow (1984)
Best of the Balkans River Cruise Launch Promotion, The Times (16 January 2021)

Singed Whiskers and Coffee

'I expected death, as much from our own men
as from the enemy, was much singed by our fire,
my whiskers twice or thrice'.

But that's to come. It's the last night of 1842 in India
and the stars are salt, cast across black ice.
Charles James Napier sits at a folding table
muffled in a cloak, boots eased off. He has a sharp nose
with spectacles and sprouts hair like marram grass.

Below, in the valley, his army's camp fires
blister the night. Baggage camels snort and grumble.
He prods the embers and fills his cup again
from a pot shaped like a pear. 'One night I drank strong coffee
and had a capital think for an hour.

I got many matters decided'. He will drag
two cannon through the ruthless desert,
take the fort of Emanghur, smithereen its walls,
then press on for Hyderabad. The Amirs will fight fiercely
but Sindh will fall. Controversial, then and now.

Our coffee pot is silver touched with tarnish.
Its pear-shaped form bursts with Rococo
flowers and a spout curved as a peacock's neck.
It's known the scrum and scuff of time but was it his?
My godmother, fast-witted and with a ready laugh,

gave us the pot, hinted at its tale and told us Charles
was said to be her ancestor. Its hallmarks,
an ornate C and Leopard Head Crowned,
prove that it was made in 1758. I catch a scent
as acrid as a jackal and hunt through Charles' family tree,

Butler's biography and Project Gutenberg.
Only then do I dig out the letter from my Aunty
and grasp the link 'I shall make up a story for the boys
that it was used by General Sir Charles Napier'.
Facts sink into the desert sands, my Aunty winks.

Part 4

Caravaggio never painted

a young man on the run
but he slips through every canvas.

In Milan the artist ground colours,
stabbed a man and fled. Rome took
him in, gave him board and bed

and a smoke-thin chance
to scrabble for religious gold.
His style was brave, light

framed with deepest pitch,
the disciples balding, old
with naked muddy feet, made real.

Death of the Virgin went too far,
a courtesan for Mary's face,
true grieving friends, no glory.

Rejected altarpiece.
He's back, strutting on the streets,
sword at his side, a slug of wine.

The duel is flicker-quick,
a clean thrust through the thigh,
Tomassoni's line bleeds out.

He flees to Naples. His style
turns darker still, no mid-tones,
his Jesus weary, without spark.

Sails for Sicily where
he sleeps in all his clothes
but Tomassoni's men

grab him and give the bill,
crunch his hand and carve
his face up through an eye.

On the edge of his final scene
he paints his own face:
ice-white, staring, still.

Melancholy

Me, under the mauve blanket,
anaesthetising another afternoon
with podcast Composer of the Week,

evaporating my self-esteem
like a dew pond burned
to clay crud and scum. Yet

melancholy lets me feel
the slow peel of the day, echoes
beyond my earphone caves,

abrades the slick spiel
of 50 things to see before you die,
none of them to savour here and now.

Dark bile humour to balance
blood, phlegm and choler.
Blue's a barbarian tint, it's wode.

Perhaps if I have stumbled such fog
I can travel with bewildered men
with drabness in their eyes,

learn that the ebb is strung
with the flow, that winter's pause
prepares the sight for spring.

Melancholy: disorder to be cured,
symmetry maintained, acceptance of
how much pain we pass through?

Shoelace of thought

My shoelace starts
in a half-dark room
filled with the thrum
of spinning wheels
in bashed green metal.

A tang of leather and grease,
it's the cobblers on London Road
with me, shorts age,
and Mum, somewhere,
not in shot.

My Dad and I
weave through the
plastic beauty women
and sickly scent
of the Army and Navy Stores.

Are we buying a present?
I forget.
He's still taller than me
in his greatcoat and
flat-cap from Cleethorpes.

I remember
he knows, from just the
first few notes, that the store
is playing Beethoven's 7th.

Four decades on
in a restaurant:
all bare bulbs
and Instagram.

I'm eating 'dirty fries'
on a slim steel table
with our jumble of kids
swept from Mum's house

while my wife and sister
clear its history,
the trinkets and the junk,
so we can sell her home.

Dad is a long remembered ache
and Mum's constant presence
is now a space which I reach for
with a half-frayed shoelace of thought.

Six suited men

carry gentle Bruno, early, to his grave.
Although I cannot pray
I face this loss with a Mass'
deep-grained rhythm.

That night I shout at God.
To pray is to punch God's guts.
He did not stop the Ford
that crushed his bike, and life.

Pray for me who gave
the cash so he could own that bike.
For me, alone, who sees his mum,
face eroded by grief, reach and hold my hand.

One good foot

Most residents sit disconnected
as I wheel Mum towards the garden,
others watch TV on Volume 10 and
only Dave's room spills chatter.

A photo shows him in the amber
of a cycling team, still wiry fit at 60.
Ten years later and his right arm and leg
are listless, face half crumpled.

His words fumble so I lean close.
'They were born last week,'
three budgie chicks tumbled in down,
painted adults sing nearby.

Three weeks later, when Mum is dying,
I just discern 'How is your mother?'
and see his cobalt eyes are moist.
Dave squeezes my arm.

He moves his wheelchair slowly but
when Douglas, who's 102, needs help
Dave pushes them both
with his one good foot.

Held

A pea:
not quite
a sphere,
smoother
than the moon.

One side's a
shade darker,
a shadow that
could hide
an ant.

Pea tucked,
snug, held
in one curve
of its long
pale case.

My sister
in red and white
banded T shirt,
gappy smile,
bountiful, tangled hair.

Gar
on her garden seat:
purple dress,
smudged half-spectacles,
hearing-aid wires,

gnarled hands
with birch
bark skin,
eyes soft
with love.

I flick out
one pea,
note it fall
and pause,
held in this vivid
now.

Skull Talks
'St Jerome Writing' by Caravaggio

My work? I'm a full time paper weight.
Truth be told, I like the role.
It's simple. Nature pulls down my head.
For this I get a roof and dusting.

I don't miss food. To have to bite
and chew and grind is to risk
to chip a tooth, but heady wine -
that was fun. My shape is redefined:

no more jowls, I'm rather sleek.
What about Jerome? We didn't start
off well. He mumbled as he wrote,
a doggerel Latin, Cicero never spoke

such words, he'd have spat them out.
Jerome overflowed his space but now
we have a border and this is my book.
Worst of all was his blaze. It took

my rest away, his halo dazzled
even as he slept. I regret
losing eyelids. He's turned down
his halo now. Saves the rows,

the times I'd spook his sleep.
These days we're worn in, as one.
And like old friends, I note, each night
we look more and more alike.

A pew, a pillar and you

I clutch what I want to say,
note my stomach tense
with fear that I'll slip
into silence like a trout drifting
with the flow into the shallows.
'I have a voice. Hear me!'

So, as we climb the lane,
I share that I've written
Chapter 8 of Flourish,
started Thriving Leadership,
divided my poems by theme.
Precious but self-polished.

The air is stung with cold,
the light, cut grey as if the sun
has wandered south and out of sight.
Hawthorn blossoms
have lost their fiery lustre
and blackthorn may never bud.

You can tell the thorns apart,
discern the Black Cap's warble
and know that Beeching's Cuts
brought the railway line,
set up for ten-coached trains,
to weed-strewn, trackless sleep.

We find ourselves at either end
of a walnut pew in St Johns.
I lean against a pillar, idling my eyes
over the arched fingers of the roof
and start to share into the unhurried space
you hold. 'It's hard,' my precious wife's

Long Covid. After a decade
of chronic fatigue,
migraines and loss,
she had a clear call to priesthood
yet those spring shoots
have not survived the frost.

As I slow and dare to speak,
my crafted poetic words fail
and all that's left is me
with common pain, tears
behind my eyes and you, my friend.
A pew, a pillar and you.

One sack for Sigele
Malawi in a famine

Edged with a murmur
of fishermen, the lake burns
with fragments of sun.
Nearby, maize plants tilt,
blanched and bereft of cobs.
The staple crop has failed.

We bring four sacks of maize
to this, our guard Chiso's village.
The huts are smartly thatched,
smooth walls daubed with black
flowers, a boat, red waves.
Here they can fish the lake,

are close to market, better off
than most. The women ululate
till the flour is out, then their hands writhe,
fast as snakes, to scoop, grasp and live.

Three more jumbled hours by pickup
take us to the village of Yakobe,
our other guard. The stone-stumbled
track runs out on a mountain slope.
His people sweat life with a few knobbly goats,
draped umber by the dust.

The sunlight has the kiss
of molten metal on my skin.
They welcome us with gentle smiles.
Our four sacks of maize
are softly parcelled out. Boys in shorts
scatter with cupfuls along the paths.

They leave one whole sack for Sigele,
a widow with a twisted foot.
The sack is left, lent on a hut.
Priceless and unguarded.

Of touch
Northern Kenya

Old Thomas treads
carefully, senses the land
with his toes. His eyes
are smeared with white.

He's swathed in the crimson cloak
of the Samburu tribe. Once a warrior,
now he holds my hand. I feel
the warmth of a culture
unafraid of touch. We pray

and our worlds are briefly one, the words
of brothers whispered to our King. We talk
of last year's drought that turned
his goats from flesh and milk
to bone and dust.

'Such droughts were once in an elder's life,
then every twenty years, then ten and five.

Have we caused this? Is God punishing us
for fighting with the Rendille?
We cut down the mwangati cedars
for charcoal, to cook. They can
no longer trap the clouds.'

Old Thomas will never see the buzzing neon of Beijing
or muffle himself against the aircon-ice of Miami's massive airport.
He will never travel in a plane, sleek with light.
What kind of brother am I if I am part of this?

Old Thomas waves me into his hut: a dome
of arched sticks and stretched food bags
with English words in UN blue.

My eyes stream from the smoke in the dark.
We drink sharp tea till I need to leave.
He spits a blessing on my hand.

Acknowledgements

- 'Painting with Darkness and Light' was first published in *Rust and Moth* (Winter, 2021);
- 'Mutation' was first published in *Time and Singing* (Fall, 2021);
- 'Awake' was first published in *Cannon's Mouth: 80* (2021);
- 'Bluebell and Leaf' was first published in *Only in the Shadow,* Mole Valley Poets' Anthology (2020);
- 'Periphery' was first published in *New Contexts: 3*, Coverstory books (2022);
- 'Malawi, Famine, Gunshot' was first published in *Saraswati: 66* (2022);
- 'Seeing Colour' was first published in *Saraswati: 66* (2022);
- 'A Peculiar Pint' was first published & displayed at The Hunter's Inn;
- 'Motherwell's Muse' first appeared in *Poetry Worth Hearing* (Summer, 2022);
- 'Riddle from the Sands' was first published in *Orbis: 198* (2020);
- 'Shoelace of Thought' was first published in *Cannon's Mouth: 80* (2021);
- 'A Pew, Pillar and You' was first published in *Friends and Friendship Anthology*, volume 2, The Poet (2021);
- 'One Sack for Sigele' was first published in *Sky Island Journal* (2021);
- 'Of Touch' was first published in *Saraswati: 66* (2022).

About the author

Richard Lister works alongside local people to tackle poverty in East Africa, South Asia and the UK. His work is published in a range of international publications including *Orbis*, *Shooters Literary Magazine*, and *Ekphrastic Review*. Lister's poetry is also carved into the Radius sculpture and is audio-exhibited at the Watts Gallery.

www.ingramcontent.com/pod-product-compliance
Lightning Source LLC
Chambersburg PA
CBHW030044100526
44590CB00011B/323